Calman at the Royal Opera House

CALMAN
AT THE
ROYAL
OPERA
HOUSE

J. M. Dent & Sons Ltd.
LONDON

by the same author

But it's my turn to leave you... *(Methuen)*
How about a little quarrel before bed? *(Methuen)*
It's only you that's incompatible *(Methuen)*
My God *(Aurum Press)*
What else do you do? *(Methuen)*
Calman at the movies *(The Bodley Head)*

First published 1990
© Mel Calman 1990

Printed in Great Britain by
Guernsey Press Co. Ltd, Guernsey, C.I.
for J. M. Dent & Sons Ltd
91 Clapham High St
London SW4 7TA

British Library Cataloguing in Publication
Data is available upon request.

ISBN 0 460 86047 X

To everyone at the Royal Opera House who bravely carried on while I got in their way.

Introduction

On my first morning at the Royal Opera House, I settled down in the stalls with a fresh sketchbook and sharpened pencils, just in time to see most of the chorus suddenly leave the ground and rise up to the flies – all the time singing away as if this was the normal way to rehearse opera. The opera was 'Un re in ascolto' and I still don't know why they had to fly.

The same morning I went up to the Opera Rehearsal Room to watch Herr Schaaf rehearsing 'Così fan tutte', where there was a bit more respect for the laws of gravity.

For the next few months, I had the freedom to wander about to listen, look and try to capture some of the Opera House's special atmosphere on paper. The place is like a village – a complete community where everyone knows everyone else. Part of the charm of the village is that so many of the inhabitants have been there a long time. About 120 people (out of 1300) have been at Covent Garden for over 20 years. Someone who has been there for nine years called himself 'a new boy'. I was impressed by the hard graft that goes into opera and ballet – so many people, so much sweat.

One of my favourite places was the canteen, where there was always a rich mix of stage staff and artists in costume. There's something irresistible about watching a man in armour from 'Il Trovatore' ordering egg and chips.

I saw men and women in sweaters and trainers pretending to be kings and princesses. I saw Placido Domingo waiting in the wings and talking football scores with his fellow gypsies. Vestal virgins wondered where they would go for their summer hols and whether pasta was really fattening. A beautiful young dancer wished she had time for a pee before the curtain went up and she became a cygnet.

And all the time I heard wonderful music all round me. I tell you, it's a hard way to make a living.

Mel Calman

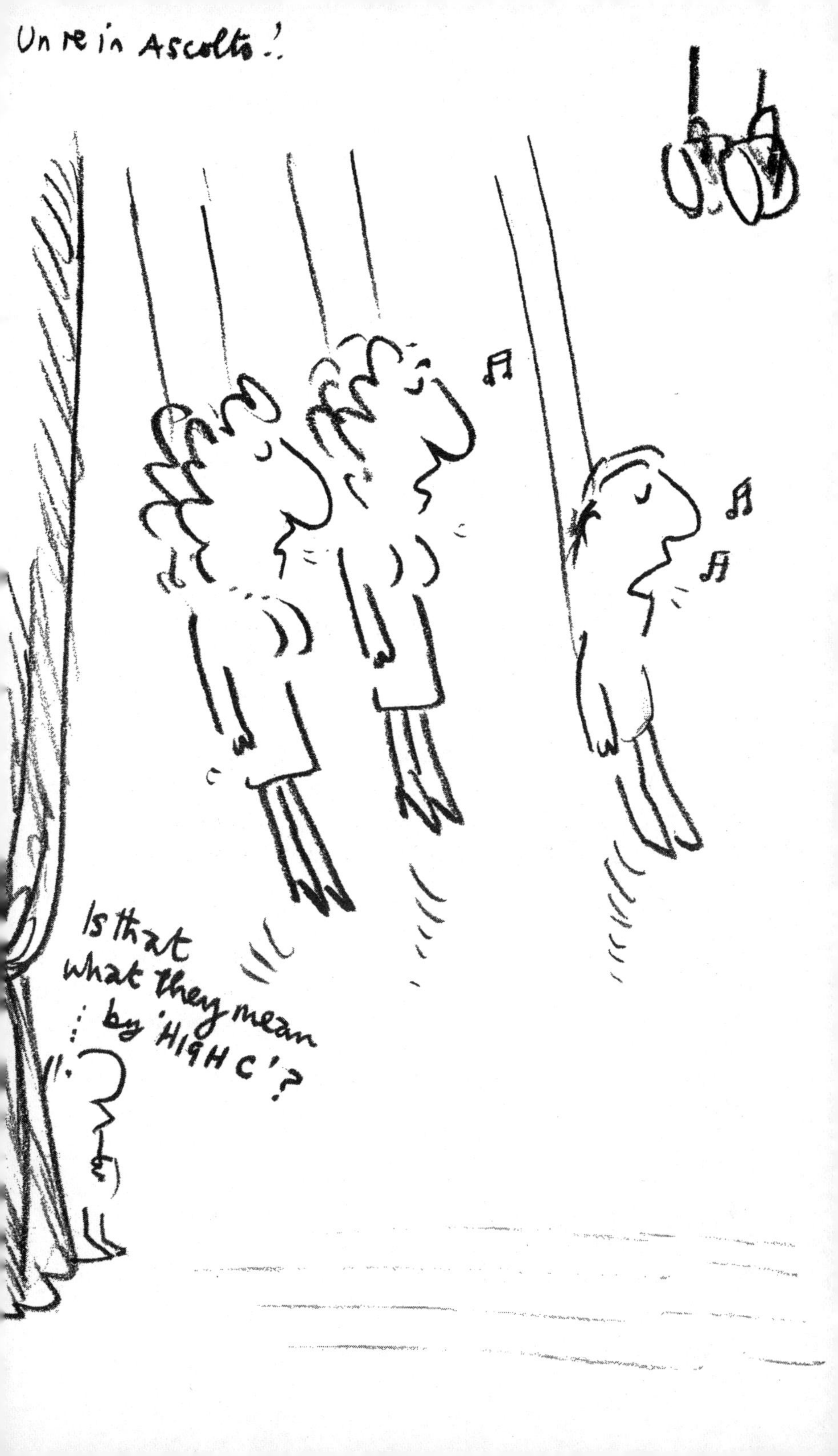
Un re in Ascolto!
Is that what they mean by 'HIGH C'?

Costume
Dept.

Sewing a ballet
skirt..

SINGER

Costu...
from
'Un re...
As col...

Caliban

Tree →

Don't give ME
that FISHY look

Fishman ↑

'N RE IN ASCOLTO' by BERIO —
...bera about a DIRECTOR
...hearsing THE TEMPEST · (I think)...
...here's TRAPEZE ARTISTS, a MAN CUTTING a woman in half,
a FISH couple, a BIRDMAN and a
great deal of CHAOS..

Cosi - rehearsal

Producer's table.
Johannes Schaaf —
and Jeffrey Tate...

Lots of
Normburgs...
cushions

Cosi - rehearsal

Johannes
Schaaf

Susanne
(DORABELLA)
waiting..

Large masks
with RED silks
↓ coming out of mouths.

A ghoulish moment
in TURANDOT...

A bit of
SKULLDUGGERY?

TURANDOT-

Calaf-
Tenor
in cardigan-
looking like
an Italian
restaurant
owner on his
day off--

DANCERS..

Nice new suit

TURANDOT rehearsal

The Princess
rehearsing
in sweater & skirt.
The executioner then
enters in a BROWN WOOL
cardigan..

ALL women
are RIDDLES..

TURANDOT –
costume designs
by Sally Jacobs...

Why worry about her
name – what's her
PHONE
number?

The Princess – 'TURANDOT'
Black clouds
on Red Silk...

Rehearsing 'Sleeping Beauty'..
Waiting to go on..
My left shoe's TOO small..
Back with 11, Steve!
Come in on the TABS, John..
Arthur - TRIM THE GAUZES!
DAILY

A. Dowell
swathed in a
dressing gown

sweater
around waist.
like UMPIRES
at cricket matches..

Monica Mason: Assistant to Anthony Dowell,
                Director of The Royal Ballet.

'Dancers must go to practice class every day for an
hour. It can't be done at home - it must be done
with a teacher, a barre, a wooden floor and music.
I've done it regularly since I was about 16 until
I was about 42. I now exercise when I'm teaching
classes. You hate it sometimes - but you always
feel better for it. It gets rid of a lot of
rubbish. It's good to focus on one thing. Margot
Fonteyn told me that when her husband was shot and
it was an awful period in her life, the only thing
that kept her sane was doing her daily practice.
During that hour she could forget everything.
        It's hard for dancers because they're racing
against the clock. They have a very short working life - about 15 years - and if they haven't
made it by the time they're 25, they won't. It's
not like actors who can go on to play character
roles.
        Dancers have to recognize and come to terms
with what their talents are. What your body is -
what you look like. If you want to be a classical
dancer, you need a certain kind of body. Great
dancers are rare - and great choreographers even
rarer.
        At present we have two young black students
in the Ballet School. We would very much like to
have more, both in the School and the Royal Ballet
Companies, and are working towards it.
        I've noticed that dancers become used to
looking at themselves all the time in mirrors.
They depend on it. I try to make them dance some
of the time opposite a wall without any mirrors,
because they dance differently then. A real
audience is not the same as a mirror.
        You've got to be hungry for the theatre and
the life. You can see it in their eyes - when
they have it.'

"Its' funny—but as soon as you see a pretty young DANCER—you become very interested in CULTURE."

K.M." When it's in your body,
it'll be alright - it's
not even in your HEAD yet
Darcey." Oh (Laughs) - it is - really!

All black
sweater etc..

Kenneth Macmillan
rehearsing
'Prince of the Pagodas'.
with Jonathan Cope &
Darcey Bussell

Russell
and Cope...

≡ Faggioni (ANGRY) —
"Is a BIG EVENT - a spy comes.
Please a REACTION! After two weeks
rehearsal - how can you STILL NOT REACT!!
PLEASE!!"

A sudden plea (in German)
from singer-
"I cannot sing if the
ROPE is too tight."

IL TROVATORE —

Act I - IL TROVATORE,

Pretend gypsies
on pretend rocks —
(supported by scaffolding)

The chorus rehearsing
in shorts, swords and trainers..

I asked Placido Domingo who was
clad in ARMOUR; "What happens if
you want to scratch yourself?"
"I have to ask one of these soldiers
to scratch for me..."
(That's REAL STARDOM - getting someone
else to do your scratching).

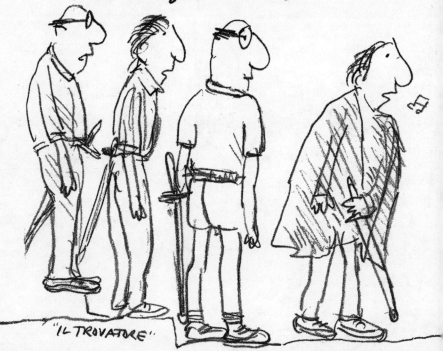

"IL TROVATORE"

IL TROVATORE:

The gypsy fire on stage –
it's not BUTANE GAS – the fire people
wouldn't approve of it, so it's NATURAL GAS –
straight from the mains. You can cook on it...

It's EGGS and BACON
: for 45 people again..

Stagehands carrying a piece of the mountain.

The awesome majesty of the TROVATORE set...

and the STAGEHANDS trying to build it...

John — can you find something to put over this hole or someone is going to break their fucking neck...

Janice Pullen is the Head of Wardrobe Dept. with
a staff of around 100 people.

'I've been here for 12 years. I was born and
brought up in Glyndebourne, where my father was
Technical Manager and my Mum was in Props. For
this job you need gut instincts, a sense of humour
- coupled with a sharp tongue and a photographic
memory. I've done five Figaros, five different
Flutes and four Macbeths - and I can remember
everything they all wore. What singers like about
Covent Garden is that there's no forelock tugging.
They feel comfortable here. I'm a bit like a nurse
treating a patient - they have their anxieties and
worries. They come off stage and perhaps the cond-
uctor or the director has criticized them and they
say - it didn't go well because there's something
wrong with the bodice. I know there's nothing wrong
with the bodice, but I soothe them and take the
bodice away and perhaps not even alter it - but
bring it back later and everything's now fine.'

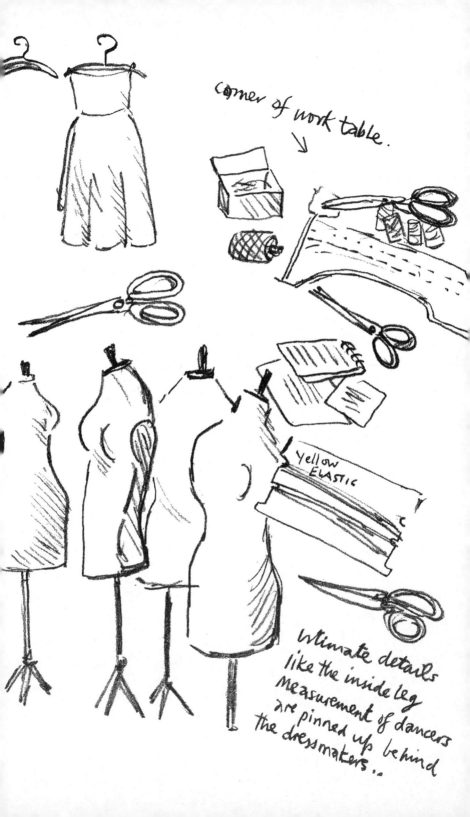

corner of work table.

Yellow
Elastic

Intimate details
like the inside leg
measurement of dancers
are pinned up behind
the dressmakers ..

Pictures on wall of dancers

window ↓

↑ Skirts

Quiet & peaceful after the noise of the rehearsal. The BURR-BURR of a sewing machine. A woman talking to someone on the phone—

Pictures everywhere—
Pinned up of mostly ballet
dancers & some
singers...

FAN

Der Rosenkavalier

Strauss: "Der Rosenkavalier"...

Over at The Royalty Theatre
they're rehearsing Der Rosenkavalier.
There's a PIANO - naked lights - paper cups - tea cups -
  sandwiches strewn on tables & floors -
the whole paraphernalia of rehearsals.
People going in the wrong directions - being told
to move somewhere else - "The calmer you are -
  the FUNNIER it will be" - pieces of advice
litter the stage ...

Royalty Theatre...
June '89

"No talking please":
to the CHORUS,
who are giggling
like school kids
in the end of term
play."

Roman
sword

←

What the well-dressed singer is wearing —
Designer jacket, jeans, trainers & a sword...

Sheet as TOGA...

La Clemenza —

Wally Bridges: Senior Barman.

'I came here in 1946. I've been here for 44 years.
When I first started I got £4 a week and champagne
was 25 bob a bottle. Champagne is now £29 a bottle
and I get £110 a week. In those days I was a
waiter in the day - I had the two jobs. Everyone
dressed up to come here then - dinner jackets,
the lot. I've had other offers, but I've stayed
here. I like the variety - every night is different. On a good night, there's a buzz in the
Crush bar, it's like a good party.

I've got my regulars - they're like friends.
Some of them treat you very well at Christmas.
One man gives me a side of smoked salmon and
chocolates for the wife. Some people tip - the
average is about 50p. But not everyone. If
everyone gave me 50p, I'd be a rich man.

One couple come here two nights a week -
and always eat here. They drink two bottles of
wine between them and six bottles of mineral water.
They also go to the ENO. It's their hobby. I
don't think they do anything else. I don't know
what they'll do when we close in '93 - some of
my regulars worry about that.

I've had regulars coming for years and then
their children come. You see couples coming
here and then if they split up or one dies, then
the other one comes less or even stops coming.
I suppose it reminds them too much of the other one.

I've another regular who has a box, and comes
four of the five nights a week. If he doesn't
use the box, then perhaps friends or his chauffeur
use it.

The two crowds are very different. The ballet
crowd are younger, and not so polite. Bit more
pushing and shoving.

I like going to the opera. We see most things.
My wife also works here. She's an usherette. But
she's only been here 26 years.

I don't like crowds. When I go out to a restaurant, I like somewhere nice and quiet. I wouldn't
like to eat here, with everyone crushing round you,
all talking and smoking. Not my idea of a treat.'

Where shall we eat afterwards?

And a
Smoked
Salmon..

Callas, of course..   Domingo..   2 bottles of champagne..

DARLING!   DARLING!   Gin and TONIC please!
                                                 oh please!

                              Dry white
                              wine

Crush bar...

The Interval...

an teen:

Madame
Butterfly
chorus eating
fish and chips

NO SMOKING

My wife said.
you don't
have to
wash the
NAPPIES,
do you?
....

Prompt corner.

Tuner

TV

Score

Phone

EXIT

Man alone in the stalls..

Stella - chief stage manager..

Stella - all knowing..

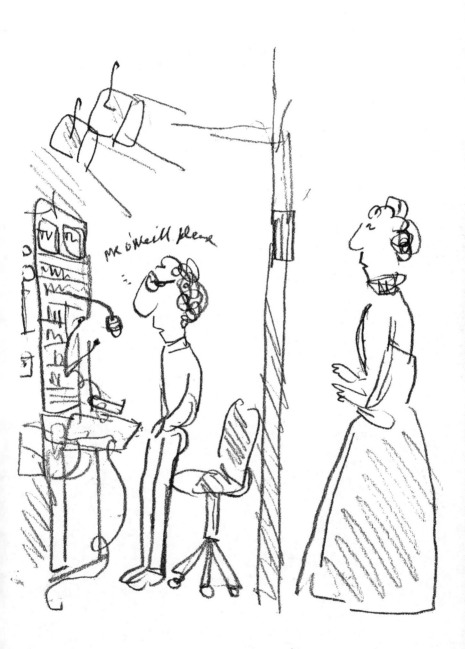

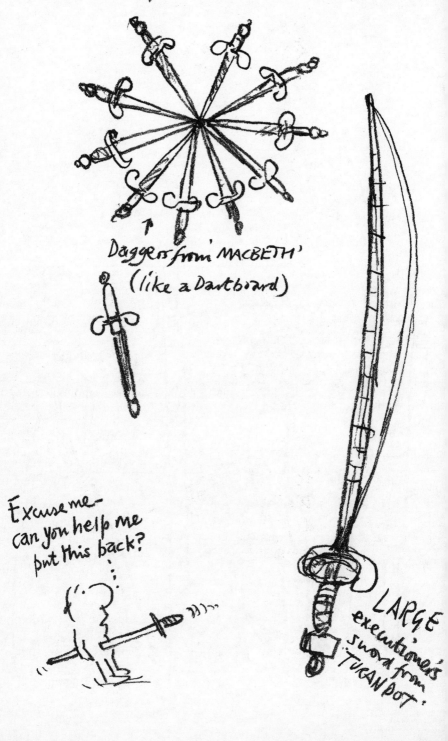

THE ARMOURY—

Daggers from 'MACBETH'
(like a Dartboard)

Excuse me—
can you help me
put this back?

LARGE
executioner's
sword from
'TURANDOT'.

The ARMOURY

Stereo radio

Plants growing out of OLD TIN HATS hanging from the skylight..

SINGER

As well as LBC on the radio - on all the time - there's the sound of the ORCHESTRA coming from the tannoy speaker

sword waiting to be cleaned

Elektramodel

striplight ↓

Plan chest

The model room: up on the 4th floor across the
street from the Opera House.

Five people work there. Colin Maxwell, the
Head of the Department, says, 'It's the biggest
in Europe.' Models usually take 2-3 weeks,
although Colin has made one in 3 days - working
all night. Colin has been here for 9 years.

'William Tell' model in a working box.

Black

'I'm a new boy - some people have been at Covent Garden for 25 years.'

The Department has two working boxes, which are complete with real lights and flying systems.

The large room is like a child's dream with its tiny props displayed in these toy sets.

Will you sign my programme?

Dancer waiting
for Igor.

Elektra rehearsal - with Sir Georg Solti -

Mino

Sloping metal floor.
(But like the Northern line Underground

White of
bra →
showing

The set has been moved
from the stage to the ORR
(Open Rehearsal Room) for the
afternoon...

Elektra dancers resting during rehearsal.

Touching up
Make up ..

Rehearsing
Elektra'..

DANCERS
waiting ..

Karen Stone: one of the resident producers.

'I began as a singer then moved into directing.
I always was moving out front to see what the
overall picture looked like - even when I was singing.
We work here for about 35 weeks in the year
and get time off to work elsewhere.
I assist the producers on new productions
and I also help revive productions that I have
worked on. We keep a large book, with photos,
and notes - not only of the moves but also of the
producers intentions and reasons. It's often more
important to know the motives behind a singer
moving, than just how the move went.
At the ENO I was often working with young
singers who were singing the role for the first
time, so that they were making a journey of dis-
covery in the role. Whereas here, you have
singers who may have sung it 200 times before and
have done the ground work, and will quickly accept
or discard your ideas and suggestions.
I'm adducted to the theatre. I love those
tingling moments when your skin prickles and it's
suddenly magical. It's thrilling when you know
you've helped the singers - in some way - to
give a great performance. That's very satisfying.
I love the element of spectacle in opera -
when the chorus come on to the stage and there's
a mass of people and energy and sheer sound.
To make terrible racist generalisations; the
German producers are methodical and suddenly given
to shouting and screaming - which can be frightening. Whereas an Italian like Faggioni, who also
shouts, isn't frightening. He does it to charge
himself up with adrenalin and will shout at the
person nearest. And that's often his assistant -
me. So the best thing is to get out of the way
just before it happens.'

Behind the huge curtain...

Come in with the tabs, JOHN!

The Wigs and Make-up
department is run by
Ron Freeman - the Wig
Master. There are ten
people working there,
serving all three comp-
anies.

'I've given 28 years
of my life to this place.
I sang as a kid in the
chorus here and then
started in this depart-
ment, making the tea and
sweeping up. In 1970 I
left to join the National
Theatre for three years,
but I missed the live
music. I was offered a
job to come back, so I
did. Everything jells
beautifully here. Of
course, there are tens-
ions sometimes, but
we're not allowed to show
them because we're here
to help the artists. Part
of us is going on that
stage.'

WIG.MAKER.

WIG MAKING

Boxes of wigs -
labelled

'I'm here from 8-8.30 in the morning
and when there's a performance till
10.30 or so at night. In all these
years, I've never felt like I didn't
want to go to work. I'm lucky.

We see the artists at their most
vulnerable - getting ready to go on.
We see them with their knickers down.
In all these years I've only had three
troublemakers - one woman and two men.
It's usually a mixture of fear and
arrogance. I've had rows, of course.

I come here from Hackney and no-
one else in my family has been in the
theatre. My father was Head Park
Keeper in Victoria Park. When I
started here, at 15, he said: "Enjoy
yourself - but beware of men with weak
handshakes."

If all this blew up tomorrow and
I didn't have this place to go to -
I don't know what I'd do.'

Real hair for
the wigs comes from
CHINA, India &
Italy...

Banner

'OTELLO' - 1990

Members of the Chorus
pretending to be
Italian peasants ..

STAGEHAND:

"Anyone who designs these sets should be made to fucking work here for two years and have to move them around. That would teach them"...

'OTELLO'

Otello & Desdemona.
Rehearsing in slightl[y]
unromantic clothes.

'otello' —

cannon

Pat Symon: Member of the chorus.

'My day starts at 6-6.30 when my daughter Nicola
wakes and wants to play. "Let's do some acting".
Her father sleeps on.
7.00 Husband gets ready for work. Try to remember all the things to be done.
8.00 Breakfast for children. Drive to school and
playgroup.
9.40 Catch train to Waterloo.
10.20 Cup of tea in canteen. Rehearsal starts at
10.30. Either music and words in Italian, German,
French, Russian, Czech, or even English sometimes,
or Production (requiring to be a nun, prostitute,
peasant, princess, maiden etc).
12.00-12.15 Tea break. Often eat lunch now to save
time later.
13.00-13.30 Rehearsal ends. Back across Waterloo
Bridge. Train home.
14.00-14.30 Relieve nanny of daughter. Shopping,
collect dry cleaning etc. Cooking evening meal
for everyone.
15.00-15.30 Collect Graham (son) from school.
16.00 Deal with charity raffle tickets/fund rais-
ing etc.
17.00 Tea for nanny and children. Sometimes join
them.
18.00 Leave by car for work. Drive takes an hour.
Fight for parking space with audience.
19.00 Sign in. Quick cup of tea. Make up, wig
and costume on ready for 7.25 first call to stage.
23.00 Home. See husband for half an hour. if he's
still awake - and it's another day gone.
     As well as this I'm studying for a City and
Guild tutor training course in Music and Drama,
leading to a degree. There's homework to be done.
And I'm rehearsing for a charity cabaret to raise
money for cancer wards.
     Take-home pay: £211 per week. 5 weeks
holiday.'

Percussion - Salome rehearsal...

Peter Morrell, Associate Stage Manager.

'I had a puppet theatre when I was six years old -
and wrote plays for it. Then I studied music and
stage management at RADA and wrote lots of letters
and finally was offered a job here. I've been
here 20 years - I joined on the 1st June 1970.
The most important part of my job is - information.
Making sure that people know things.
        Everyone in the theatre needs to be a psychol-
ogist. There are hundreds of egos - all of them
important. They all need to be considered.
        There is a considerable tension backstage.
There's a one-minute thirty-second scene change
before the last act of "Meistersinger" and we
recently had to do that. And I got the terrible
tummy runs on the technical rehearsals. It was
purely psychosomatic - because as soon as it was
over, it disappeared. In fact, if I don't have
the colley-wobbles on the first night, I worry.
You need that adrenalin.
        There is a wonderful mystery about being
behind the scenes. When I was a kid and went to
the panto I used to love seeing the glimpses of
men standing in the wings. (It's a mystique that's
almost religious.) My father wasn't in the theatre
- he ran away to join a jazz band - but he was a
Mason, and I reckon he liked the dressing-up part
of that, which is a kind of theatre.
        If this place were a factory, then it's great
to hear the customers applauding the product.
That's very satisfying.
        I enjoy going to the opera - and go as often
as I can. I saw "Elektra" three times, even though
I wasn't working on it. You mustn't get cynical
about the stage effects because you know how it's
done. I still lose myself in the piece, when I'm
just in the audience. Although I remember seeing
the ENO production of "Hansel and Gretel" and
worrying about the children cavorting around all
those trap doors, and thinking of the problems
that would cause. '

corner of PROP ROOM —

Ropes

Ladder

ROH

O.P.

Rosin Box

Jeremy Isaacs, General Director.

'I don't have a musical background, although my
mother who was a doctor did sing in student
cabaret.

Every day here there's a mixture of things
you know are going to happen and things you don't
know are going to happen. It's live theatre -
there's an electricity about it, that I enjoy.

My function is to provide the space to let
great people do great work. My one regret is that
so much of my time is spent with housekeeping -
finding money.

I'm determined to keep Covent Garden as one
of the great opera houses in the world.

I'm working longer hours than I've ever worked
before. I watch out front about three nights a
week - and also try to find the time to see the
other theatres in London. This week there are
three different productions in the house; there's
a big recital, there are two productions in
rehearsal and there's the ballet on tour in New
Zealand and Birmingham.

It takes time to settle in here. I'm
beginning to be accepted, I like to think. I'm in
charge of a wonderful sweetie shop - and I
sometimes feel I must be dreaming.'